BRAVE THE BIOME

ARCTIC AND ANTARCTIC SURVIVAL GUIDE

[SARAH EASON]

CRABTREE
PUBLISHING COMPANY
WWW.CRABTREEBOOKS.COM

BRAVE THE BIOME

Author: Sarah Eason

Editors: Jennifer Sanderson
and Ellen Rodger

Proofreader and indexer: Tracey Kelly

Proofreader: Petrice Custance

Editorial director: Kathy Middleton

Design: Jessica Moon

Cover design: Tammy McGarr

Photo research: Rachel Blount

**Production coordinator
and Prepress technician:**
Tammy McGarr

Print coordinator: Katherine Berti

Consultant: David Hawksett

Produced for Crabtree Publishing by Calcium

Photo Credits
t=Top, c=Center, b=Bottom, l= Left, r=Right

Inside: Jessica Moon: pp. 17b, 29t; Shutterstock:
ArtMari & Jessica Moon: p. 11t; Baibaz: p. 19t;
Creative Family: p. 24b; Gerasimov_foto_174: p. 9b;
Volodymyr Goinyk: pp. 28-29; Maksym Gorpenyuk:
pp. 18-19; Kris Grabiec: pp. 24-25; GTW: pp. 14-15bg;
Helter-skelter: p. 13b; Iryna Inshyna: p. 29b; James_
stone76: pp. 20-21; Kedardome: p. 6t; Szczepan
Klejbuk: p. 22b; Xavier Mertz: p. 21r; MP cz: p. 7b;
Mumemories: pp. 22-23, 30-31; Nikiteev_konstantin:
p. 7t; Nordroden: p. 12t; Yershov Oleksandr: p.
25t; Tyler Olson: p. 6b; Jens Ottoson: pp. 4-5, 8-9;
Outdoorsman: pp. 5t, 24r; Plprod: p. 17t; Ondrej
Prosicky: pp. 12-13; Oleksiy Rezin: p. 27b; Padma
Sanjaya: p. 23b; Vaclav Sebek: p. 25b; Sirtravelalot:
p. 16l; Smit: pp. 11b, 16-17; Valeriia Soloveva: p.
19b; Alex Stemmer: p. 32; Dan Tautan: pp. 10-11c;
Karl Umbriaco: pp. 26-27; Vitalfoto: p. 23t; Kevin
Xu Photography: pp. 10-11; Wikimedia Commons:
Internet Archive: p. 14; Xavier Mertz: p 21r.

Cover: All images from Shutterstock

Library and Archives Canada Cataloguing in Publication

Title: Arctic and Antarctic survival guide / Sarah Eason.
Names: Eason, Sarah, author.
Description: Series statement: Brave the biome | Includes index.
Identifiers: Canadiana (print) 20200285416 |
  Canadiana (ebook) 20200285521 |
  ISBN 9780778781318 (softcover) |
  ISBN 9780778781257 (hardcover) |
  ISBN 9781427125712 (HTML)
Subjects: LCSH: Wilderness survival—Arctic regions—Juvenile
  literature. | LCSH: Wilderness survival—Antarctica—Juvenile
  literature. | LCSH: Survival—Arctic regions—Juvenile literature.
  | LCSH: Survival—Antarctica—Juvenile literature. |
  LCSH: Arctic regions—Juvenile literature. |
  LCSH: Antarctica—Juvenile literature.
Classification: LCC GF86 .E27 2021 | DDC j613.6/90911—dc23

Library of Congress Cataloging-in-Publication Data

Names: Eason, Sarah, author.
Title: Arctic and Antarctic survival guide / Sarah Eason.
Description: New York : Crabtree Publishing Company, [2021] |
  Series: Brave the biome | Includes index.
Identifiers: LCCN 2020029901 (print) | LCCN 2020029902 (ebook) |
  ISBN 9780778781257 (hardcover) |
  ISBN 9780778781318 (paperback) |
  ISBN 9781427125712 (ebook)
Subjects: LCSH: Wilderness survival--Arctic Region--Juvenile
  literature. | Wilderness survival--Antarctica--Juvenile literature.
Classification: LCC GV200.5 .E23 2021 (print) |
  LCC GV200.5 (ebook) | DDC 613.6/9091989--dc23
LC record available at https://lccn.loc.gov/2020029901
LC ebook record available at https://lccn.loc.gov/2020029902

Crabtree Publishing Company

www.crabtreebooks.com   1-800-387-7650

Printed in the U.S.A./092020/CG20200810

Published in Canada
Crabtree Publishing
616 Welland Ave.
St. Catharines, Ontario
L2M 5V6

Published in the United States
Crabtree Publishing
347 Fifth Ave.
Suite 1402-145
New York, NY 10016

Published in the United Kingdom
Crabtree Publishing
Maritime House
Basin Road North, Hove
BN41 1WR

Published in Australia
Crabtree Publishing
3 Charles Street
Coburg North
VIC, 3058

CONTENTS

The Arctic Circle and Antarctica are the polar regions at either ends of Earth. The Arctic Circle is at the North Pole, and Antarctica is at the South Pole. At the poles, there are long, dark, freezing winters and short summers. The poles are the most isolated places on the planet. Despite this, more people are visiting them, and the Arctic is being mined for its **minerals**.

SURVIVING THE FROZEN REGIONS

The Arctic Circle is a huge area of frozen ice floating on top of the Arctic Ocean. The Arctic Ocean spreads across northern America, Europe, and Asia. It also includes Greenland, the world's largest island. The Antarctic is a vast region that reaches temperatures of -60°C (-76°F). **Snow blindness**, **frostbite**, and **hypothermia** are just a few of the dangers that can threaten people exploring these regions. Understanding the dangers of the polar regions can be the first step in surviving them.

EXPLORE WITH CARE

Exploring the polar regions is dangerous. The poles are very far away, and the number of people who can visit is controlled in order to protect the environment. Visitors must go with a guide who knows the **terrain** and the dangers. Someone who is not going on the trip must know the group's route and arrival date. If the group gets lost and fails to arrive back at base at the set time, the alarm can be raised.

Animals and plants that live at the poles, such as the Arctic fox, have **adapted** to the harsh conditions. For humans who find themselves stranded there, survival is not so easy. To survive, they need to be aware of the dangers and have skills that can make the difference between life and death.

Arctic fox ·······

More and more people are visiting Antarctica to experience living in an extreme **habitat**.

LOOK FOR ...

Look for the "How to Survive" and "Be Prepared" features in this book. These explain many of the techniques that people have used to survive in the Arctic and Antarctica.

Wearing the right clothing for an expedition is very important. Explorers should be neither too hot nor too cold. If they become too hot and start to sweat, this can lower their body temperature and lead to hypothermia, which can be deadly. Freezing polar winds can be dangerous. If wind gets into clothing, it replaces hot air with cold air, and can chill the skin and cause frostbite.

WEAR THE RIGHT CLOTHES

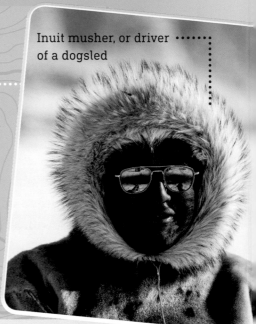

Inuit musher, or driver of a dogsled

The **Indigenous** peoples of the Arctic, such as the Inupiat of Alaska and northern Yukon, and the Inuit of Northwest Territories, Nunavut, Labrador, northern Quebec, and Greenland, wear layers. This provides **insulation** against the cold and keeps the body from becoming too hot and sweaty. Traditionally, they protected their heads with fur hoods.

THE RIGHT FOOTWEAR

The frozen ground can freeze the skin on explorers' feet, and this can lead to frostbite. Wearing proper winter hiking boots with a removable insulation layer that can be dried out is very important. Explorers wear at least two pairs of socks: thin lining socks to soak up sweat and thick woolen socks for warmth. It is important to always keep feet dry, so people must carry a spare pair of socks for sleeping in while their day pair dries out. In extreme cold, plastic bags can be wrapped around the feet under socks. This traps in heat but keeps socks from getting wet from sweat.

HOW TO DRESS TO PREVENT HYPOTHERMIA

Hypothermia is a great threat to polar explorers. To prevent hypothermia, people layer their clothes. These layers should include:

- A first layer made from a material that helps keep the body dry from sweat.
- A second layer to keep warm.
- An insulating third layer, such as a warm fleece.
- A cold-weather outdoor jacket that is windproof and waterproof.
- Explorers should also take an extra-thick jacket to wear when they stop for breaks to keep their body temperature from going down quickly.

extra-thick jacket

Travelers cover as much of their skin as possible to keep safe. Snow goggles protect the eyes from snow blindness.

WHITEOUT: FUNATSU KEIZO

Funatsu Keizo, an experienced explorer and dogsled handler, joined the Trans-Antarctica Expedition in 1989 to attempt the journey of a lifetime. He and five other explorers planned to travel across Antarctica without a motorized vehicle for the first time ever.

ALMOST THERE

The expedition's 6 men and 36 dogs had already weathered blizzards and heavy snowfall while crossing 3,741 miles (6,020 km) of the remote Antarctic. Camped for the night and with just 16 miles (25.7 km) to go before completing their mission, it looked like smooth sailing. But nothing is ever a sure bet in Antarctica.

WHITEOUT!

Funatsu awoke at 4:30 a.m. to feed the dogs on the final day. Then, he stepped out of his tent into a mass of blowing white snow. He was not far from his tent when he realized that this was a whiteout, and it could be a killer. Funatsu could barely see in front of him, and he could not retrace his footing back to camp. His only choice was to use survival skills and stay warm while he waited out the blizzard.

HOLE IN THE SNOW

As a dog handler, Funatsu knew that when it is bitterly cold, sled dogs dig a hole in the snow to curl up in, covering their nose and face with their tail to keep warm. Funatsu decided to copy this idea. He used a pair of pliers he had in his pocket to dig a shallow hole to lay down in.

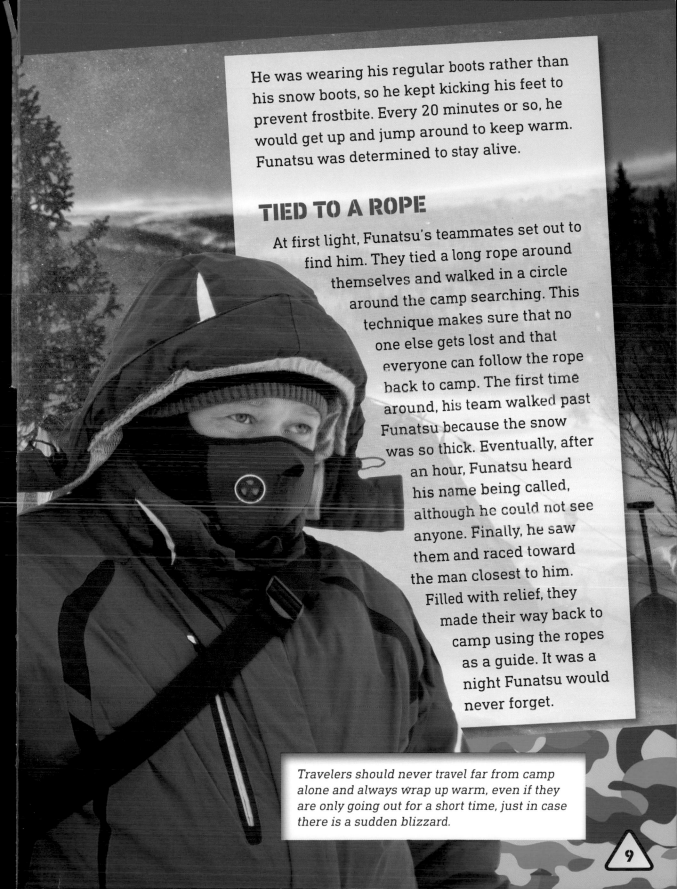

He was wearing his regular boots rather than his snow boots, so he kept kicking his feet to prevent frostbite. Every 20 minutes or so, he would get up and jump around to keep warm. Funatsu was determined to stay alive.

TIED TO A ROPE

At first light, Funatsu's teammates set out to find him. They tied a long rope around themselves and walked in a circle around the camp searching. This technique makes sure that no one else gets lost and that everyone can follow the rope back to camp. The first time around, his team walked past Funatsu because the snow was so thick. Eventually, after an hour, Funatsu heard his name being called, although he could not see anyone. Finally, he saw them and raced toward the man closest to him. Filled with relief, they made their way back to camp using the ropes as a guide. It was a night Funatsu would never forget.

Travelers should never travel far from camp alone and always wrap up warm, even if they are only going out for a short time, just in case there is a sudden blizzard.

Blizzard winds in Antarctica can reach more than 100 miles per hour (160 km/h). In some of these severe snowstorms, the swirling snow is so thick that it is impossible to see very far ahead. It is easy for explorers to get lost by becoming separated from their group or not being able to find their way back to the camp. If a blizzard is coming, the camp must be set up immediately, before the blizzard hits. People can then sit out the blizzard in their tents or other shelters.

DEADLY SNOW DUNES

Polar explorers need to be aware of ground blizzards. Even if the sky is blue and clear, strong winds can whip up the ground snow, causing it to swirl around and create whiteout conditions. When the storm has stopped, the ground can look like snow waves made up of deep grooves and sharp ridges called sastrugi. Traveling across sastrugi can be very slow, and skis and other equipment can easily be broken. If they suddenly come across sastrugi, groups need to think about **rationing** any remaining food and water they have, in case their journey takes longer than expected.

Experienced explorers remain in their tent if they believe that a storm could be on the way.

BE PREPARED

When explorers set up camp, they should build a wall of snow about 26 feet (8 m) away from their tent. The snow wall will keep the tent from being buried or blown away in a storm. The wall should be built so it is facing toward the wind.

snow wall

When pitching a tent, it is important to make sure that the tent's opening is facing away from the direction of the wind.

11

FIGHT THE FREEZE

One of the biggest dangers to polar explorers is frostbite. Frostbite happens in stages. The first stage, called frostnip, is when the skin turns pale and itches, burns, or stings. Advanced frostbite happens when the muscle and fat underneath the skin become frozen and die. To begin with, people feel painful cold in the affected areas. Then, the pain lessens, and they feel a little stiff. This is when the frostbite is actually getting worse. If it is not treated, the frostbitten area will drop off.

PREVENTING FROSTBITE

Frostbite usually affects areas that are most exposed to the cold, such as people's fingers and hands, toes in damp boots, and face. The right clothes are essential to prevent frostbite. Mittens are better than gloves and can be kept on a string that runs from the back of the neck to each hand, to keep them from being dropped or blown away in a blizzard. Wearing scarves and balaclavas will protect the whole face, especially the ears and nose. Animals, such as seals and polar bears, survive the freezing conditions thanks to their blubber. This is a layer of fat that helps keep them warm. Polar bears also have fur that insulates them.

seal

LOOK FOR SIGNS

The first signs of frostbite, especially on the face, might not even be felt. That is why explorers check each other's faces for signs of frostnip. They look for the skin turning white and waxy or red or blue. If this is happening, the affected area must be warmed up immediately by taking shelter and putting dry clothing over the area. Cold or frostbitten hands can be temporarily warmed by putting them under the armpits.

Eyelashes, lips, the nose, and cheeks can all be affected by frostbite. Travelers keep as much as possible of their face well covered.

BE PREPARED

People exploring the polar regions should always carry a survival bag with the right equipment to protect them from the extreme cold and sudden blizzards. The bag should contain:

- protein bars
- emergency space blanket
- portable shovel
- fire-starting kit
- heat packs
- small tarp or plastic sheet

protein bar

The foil-like material, of this emergency space blanket helps to trap body heat.

ALONE IN THE SNOW
ADA BLACKJACK

Ada Blackjack survived nearly two years on a remote Arctic island where her fellow travelers died on the ill-fated 1921 Wrangel Island Expedition. Using her self-taught survival skills, she is one of the few people to have survived such a long time in an extreme climate.

DESPERATE

Ada Blackjack was an Inupiat born in Spruce Creek, Alaska, in 1898. She was brought up by **missionaries** who taught her to sew and cook. The death of Ada's husband left her **destitute** with a sick five year old son. Ada was asked to join four explorers on an expedition to Wrangel Island in the Arctic Ocean. She had her doubts about the journey—the explorers were young and inexperienced—but the pay was good, and she had her son to look after.

Ada Blackjack kept a diary of her activities and took photographs of herself at the camp.

NO MORE FOOD

In 1921, the team set sail for Wrangel Island. Ada's job was to sew and cook for the men. They had enough food for six winter months, and they lived off the land during the summer, after which a supply ship would bring them food. But the ship was unable to reach them because of thick ice, and the treacherous winter set in. Their food soon ran out, and there were few animals to hunt. One of the men, Lorne Knight, was starving and sick. The other men left Knight with Ada to look for help. They were never seen again.

ADA ALONE

Ada was left to do the work of four men and look after Knight. She hunted for what little food there was, cooked, and tried to keep Knight as comfortable as possible. When Knight died, Ada stacked boxes around him to protect his body from wild animals. Although she was alone, she was determined to survive, so that she could be reunited with her son.

DETERMINED

To keep herself safe from polar bears, Ada built a lookout platform and a gun rack above her bed to shoot the animals if they came into her tent at night. She learned how to set traps to catch food and taught herself to shoot birds and seals. Ada was finally rescued in August 1923. She had survived because of her determination to see her son again, her courage, and her ability to adapt to her surroundings. Ada was never paid the money owed to her for the expedition.

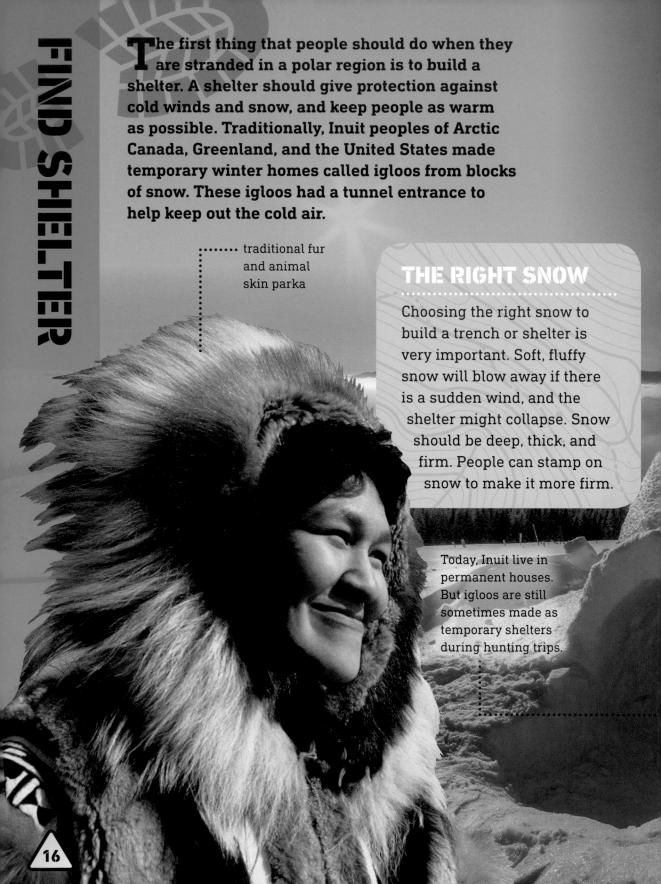

The first thing that people should do when they are stranded in a polar region is to build a shelter. A shelter should give protection against cold winds and snow, and keep people as warm as possible. Traditionally, Inuit peoples of Arctic Canada, Greenland, and the United States made temporary winter homes called igloos from blocks of snow. These igloos had a tunnel entrance to help keep out the cold air.

traditional fur and animal skin parka

THE RIGHT SNOW

Choosing the right snow to build a trench or shelter is very important. Soft, fluffy snow will blow away if there is a sudden wind, and the shelter might collapse. Snow should be deep, thick, and firm. People can stamp on snow to make it more firm.

Today, Inuit live in permanent houses. But igloos are still sometimes made as temporary shelters during hunting trips.

SIGNAL FOR HELP

If there is a strong blizzard, it is likely that rescue teams will come looking for people they know are out exploring. To alert rescuers, a bright piece of clothing is tied to a tree. An **SOS** sign can also be made with rocks or in the snow. Once a rescue signal has been made, it is important that people stay where they are and build a trench for shelter.

HOW TO BUILD A SNOW TRENCH

A snow trench is a form of emergency shelter. It can be built quickly if people find themselves stuck or stranded in the snow and cold. A trench should be longer than a person's body and wider than their shoulders. A support for the roof can be built using skis, poles, or sturdy branches laid across the trench. A tarp is then laid across the support to make a waterproof covering. This can be held in place by extra snow stamped down, rocks, or any equipment. A layer of fluffy snow is added to make it warmer, and a stick is used to make an air hole. The floor is then covered using fir or spruce tree branches, a spare blanket, or anything that will keep people's bodies off the cold ground.

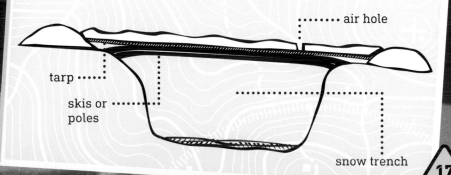

air hole

tarp

skis or poles

snow trench

Food provides the nutrients that the body needs as it works to keep warm. Food also gives people energy and keeps them alert. Energy from food is measured in calories. In polar conditions, high-calorie diets, which include foods such as protein bars and chocolate, provide energy and keep people warm. Trekkers allow for about 5,000 calories per person each day.

FREEZE-DRIED FOOD

In freezing conditions, the grease or fat in food freezes, so chocolate bars and cheese will become rock hard. Cutting cheese, chocolate, butter, and other foods rich in fat into small pieces before the trip will help them to defrost quickly. Foods eaten on polar expeditions should be easy to cook. **Freeze-dried** meals are best and easy to carry. Arctic peoples traditionally ate a lot of animal fats to give them energy. Small pieces of butter can be added to freeze-dried meals, so that when the meals are cooked, the butter will provide extra calories.

EAT SNACKS

Trekking through the snow uses a lot of energy. Eating snacks regularly throughout the day can keep up energy levels. Good snacks include dried meats such as jerky, dried fruit, nuts, seeds, and chocolate pieces.

chocolate ·······················

To keep up their energy, trekkers can try traditional snacks such as muktuk, made from whale blubber and skin, or bannock, a type of fried bread.

BE PREPARED

Drinking regularly throughout the day will help explorers stay **hydrated**. Unmelted snow should never be eaten. This is because the body will need to melt the snow to turn it into liquid. This will cause the body to lose heat, which could lead to hypothermia. The best way to melt snow is on a campfire. Pouring the water into a bottle will keep it hot. The water will then be ready for them when they set off the next day.

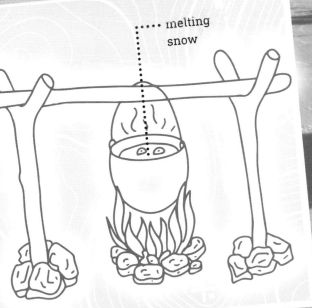

melting snow

INTO THE UNKNOWN:
DOUGLAS MAWSON

Inspired by his experience exploring the polar continent with other expeditions, Douglas Mawson spent many months making plans to conduct scientific research in unknown areas of Antarctica. In 1911, with a group of more than 30 scientists and 48 sled dogs, his Australasian Antarctic Expedition set off to explore Antarctica. It would be the most devastating journey of his life.

INTO THE WHITE

After setting up their base camp, Douglas split his team into four groups. One group would manage the camp, while the others were given scientific assignments into unknown stretches of Antarctica that would take years to finish. Douglas headed the riskiest assignment: a three-man team traveling hundreds of miles from base camp, over ground that had deep snow-covered **crevasses**. Douglas was an experienced polar explorer, but he underestimated the journey ahead and the danger of the environment. This would later cost the lives of his team.

CRACK IN THE ICE

To begin with, Douglas's journey went to plan, but after several weeks, the first disaster hit. One of the team, Belgrave Ninnis, plunged down a crevasse with his sled and two dogs. Douglas and the other team member, Mertz, crawled to the edge of the crevasse and called Belgrave's name, but there was no reply. After five hours they gave up. Since Belgrave's sled had most of the food supplies, the two men had only enough food for just over a week and no food for the dogs.

DISASTER STRIKES

The men continued on their expedition, but after a few days, Douglas became snow blind. The next disaster struck when they hit a whiteout during a blizzard, and two of their dogs died. The men attached themselves to the sled and continued as best they could. Mertz became weaker and weaker as they trudged several miles a day with very little food. Soon, he became too sick to continue. He died, leaving Douglas alone and many miles from base camp.

CLOSE TO DEATH

Douglas had severe frostbite on his feet. Although he could barely walk, he was determined to get back to base camp. As he dragged himself across the snow and ice, he suddenly found himself hanging in the air over a bottomless hole, holding onto his rope... He had fallen through a crevasse and was left gripping his rope for dear life. Slowly and painfully, he pulled himself up the rope and onto the ice. As he struggled on, he survived starvation by eating the dogs. By the time he reached base camp, Douglas was in terrible condition, but thankful he had survived.

Douglas's determination to see his fiancée again and to tell the world what had happened helped him survive.

It is essential to know how to build a fire in wilderness conditions. A fire heats food, melts snow, dries wet boots, and keeps people warm. Building a fire can also help keep wild animals away from human camps. Although many animals **migrate** or **hibernate** to avoid the harsh polar winters, some remain in the wilderness and can be a danger to humans.

CHOOSE A SPOT

Choosing a place to build a fire is very important. The fire should be protected from wind and snow, so explorers try to look for a spot next to a rock or high snow ridge. If explorers choose a spot under trees, they clear away any snow from the branches first, since the fire may melt the snow, and the melting snow will put out the fire.

Gray wolves live in Alaska, northern Canada, and other Arctic regions, such as Norway. Hungry wolves looking for food can be a danger, so campers should keep a fire burning throughout the night to keep them away.

BUILDING A FIRE

When preparing to make a fire in the snow, it is a good idea to make a pit. By digging into the snow and building a fire within it, the fire will be protected from any wind that could blow it out. It is also important to build the fire so that melting snow will not put it out. Explorers often use rocks as a base or build a platform with crisscrossing branches to keep the logs above away from any melting snow. It is important to always collect enough wood or kindling, such as twigs and bigger branches, to keep the fire going.

firepit

HOW TO MAKE A FIRE IN THE SNOW

Explorers should carry a fire-starter kit, but if they do not have one, they should look for small pieces of dry wood. This may not be easy in snowy **biomes**, so they should find the driest dead branch they can and peel away the outer layers with a knife if possible, until they reach the dry wood. Larger branches can be put on the fire before explorers go to sleep. This will keep the fire burning throughout the night.

In the Arctic, the biggest **predators** are polar bears. Polar bear attacks on humans are rare. However, as a result of **global warming**, the sea ice is melting, and polar bears are being driven into areas where humans live. Polar bears are intelligent and can outrun and outswim humans, so a person's best chance of survival against polar bears is to avoid them altogether. Arctic peoples have learned to live with polar bears by understanding them and their behavior, and treating them with respect.

KEEP AWAY

In the fall and winter, most bears hunt seals on the ice, so explorers try to keep clear of these areas. Polar bears with cubs are especially dangerous because the mother will attack if she thinks the cubs are threatened. During the summer, when the ice has melted, polar bears are forced to wander along the coastline and beaches and farther inland, searching for food. Trekkers should always keep a lookout for polar bears using binoculars to scan the land.

mother bear and cubs

Anyone exploring the Arctic must keep a lookout for bears and other dangerous animals.

BE PREPARED

Bear pepper spray or signal flares can be used to scare away bears. A course in bear awareness will help any explorer before a trip where there could be bears. These classes teach trekkers how to deal with bears without using guns.

pepper spray

SENSE OF SMELL

Polar bears are active all year round and at any time during the day, but they hunt mostly in the evening and at night. They have a strong sense of smell, so all food should be kept in containers with lids and stored at least 150 feet (45 m) from the camp. Any cooking should be done as far away from the camp as possible and any food waste buried far away from camp. It is important to avoid using anything with a strong sense of smell, such as soap and shampoo.

CHASED BY WOLVES:
PAULOOSIE KEYOOTAK

Pauloosie Keyootak cried with relief and jumped for joy when he and his son, Atamie, and nephew, Peter, were rescued after being lost on Baffin Island in the Arctic for eight days. The three Inuit men had traditional survival skills so thought the two-day journey from Iqaluit to Qikiqtarjuag would be straightforward. But modern technology let them down. They soon discovered that the Arctic can be a dangerous place, even for experienced travelers. When they hadn't arrived four days after they set out, a rescue party was sent to look for them.

THE WRONG WAY

The men set off in March 2016, planning to travel south, but a faulty **GPS** meant they went north, off their route. The men realized they had been traveling in the wrong direction when, after two days, they still had not reached their destination. They had only enough food to last two days and two small cans of fuel for their portable stove. They did not even have tents. Pauloosie had a knife with him and used it to build an igloo as a shelter. They managed to hunt two caribou for food and used their skills to skin the carcass and prepare the skins so they could use them to sleep on. They shared two sleeping bags, huddling together for warmth.

HOWLING WOLF

The men gathered branches and leaves and used the bullet cases from their guns to make a fire. They walked around the camp to keep warm. They tried to write SOS messages to mark where they were. Then, cold, scared, and running out of food, the group had to face another danger. A large wolf had found their campsite and was sniffing around. The men were too scared to go outside the camp.

They had used all their bullets to hunt the caribou and had only the knife for protection. Pauloosie attached a piece of wood to the end of the knife to make it longer, so that it would make a better weapon against the wolf if needed.

HELICOPTER RESCUE

When the men did not arrive at their destination on time, a rescue team set off, but its work was delayed by heavy snowstorms and the fact that the men had gone off course. Eventually, there was one place left to search. As they flew over the land, they saw Pauloosie on top of a hill waving at them. Pauloosie had heard the plane and rushed out to signal for help. All three men were rescued and were uninjured.

Having some knowledge of the survival techniques used by Indigenous peoples can keep explorers alive if they get lost in Arctic conditions.

The Arctic and Antarctica are some of the most challenging places on Earth to survive. However, people have lived for many months, even years, in these harsh biomes. Polar survival depends on being prepared for the unexpected and remembering not to panic, making a plan, and following the survival tips in this book.

KEEP TOGETHER

Always travel in a group. The first thing people need to do is find or make a shelter, then make a fire.

HYPOTHERMIA AND FROSTBITE

Hypothermia and frostbite are the biggest dangers in the freezing cold. It is very important to wear the right clothes and keep every bit of skin covered. Wet clothing should be changed as soon as possible. Activities that make people sweat should be avoided because sweating will make their clothes wet and when they dry out, this can lead to heat loss. Explorers must check each other for frostbite all the time.

EAT AND DRINK

Trekkers need to make sure that they have emergency rations of high-calorie food that are easy to carry, such as protein bars, dried fruit and nuts, and chocolate bars. They should melt some snow before they set off and take sips throughout the day, but avoid eating snow.

HOW TO SIGNAL FOR HELP

There are several ways to signal for help:

- If possible, make a fire using something made from rubber to create thick, black smoke.
- Build little piles of stones or twigs to show your route.
- Use a mirror, aluminum foil, or a similar shiny surface to reflect light to a passing helicopter or airplane.
- Make a large X or SOS or HELP sign on the ground using rocks or stones, but these may eventually be covered by snow.

Keeping hydrated helps the body maintain energy.

29

adapted Developed skills or physical features over time to live in a certain biome

biomes Large areas where plants and animals naturally live. A biome is also recognized by other features, such as how much water it has and what its weather is like.

crevasses Deep cracks in the ice

destitute Having no money, no possessions, and no home

freeze-dried Describes food that has all the water removed

frostbite A condition caused by extreme cold, when the muscles and tissues become frozen and the affected area drops off

global warming The gradual warming of Earth's climate

GPS An acronym for Global Positioning System, a system that uses space satellites to help people find their way

habitat The natural environment in which an animal or plant normally lives or grows

hibernate To go into a sleep in the winter, where the body slows down and feeds on its own fat

hydrated Having enough water

hypothermia When a person's body temperature becomes too low, causing serious damage

Indigenous peoples The original inhabitants of a land

insulation Something that protects against the cold

isolated Alone and far away from any other person or place

migrate To move from one place to another in search of food and shelter

minerals Substances that occur naturally in rock, sand, and soil

missionaries People who go to other countries to teach the people about a religion

predators Animals that hunt and kill other animals for food

rationing Allowing only so much per person at one time

snow blindness Temporary blindness caused by the reflection of Sun on snow or ice

SOS A universal rescue signal that stands for Save Our Souls

terrain The land and how it looks

LEARNING MORE

Find out more about the polar regions and how to survive them.

Hanel, Teresa Rachel. *Can You Survive Antarctica?: An Interactive Survival Adventure* (You Choose: Survival). Capstone Press, 2011.

Hyde, Natalie. *Expedition to the Arctic* (Crabtree Chrome). Crabtree Publishing Company, 2014.

Miles, John C. *Pathways Through Antarctica* (The Human Path Across the Continents). Crabtree Publishing Company, 2020.

Yomtov, Nel. *Explorers of the Coldest Places on Earth* (Extreme Explorers). Capstone Press, 2020.

WEBSITES

Learn about Canadian Inuit peoples and their traditions at:
www.itk.ca/about-canadian-inuit

Check out ways that people can camp safely in polar regions at:
www.msrgear.com/blog/pro-tips-for-winter-base-camping

Discover more animals that live in the polar regions at:
www.npolar.no/en/species-archive

Find extra tips on survival in the Antarctic at:
www.coolantarctica.com/Antarctica%20fact%20file/frequently_asked_questions.php

INDEX

ABOUT THE AUTHOR

Sarah Eason has written a lot of books about biomes and the animals that live in them and have adapted to survive there. On her travels, she has also visited different biomes, including oceans, forests, and snowy mountains. She has never visited the Arctic or Antarctic, but if she does, she will make sure that she uses the useful skills in this book!